Praise for Rikki Santer

"For those who may think poetry is obtuse and boring, *In Pearl Broth: Poems New & Selected* will shake that notion free. Rikki Santer's poems are chock-full of vibrant language that evokes responses in both the busy mind and the quiet heart of the reader: *piffling questions multiply like maggots . . . the mall tilts on its axis . . . we like handcuffing matters down . . . secret bag of caramels in a lingerie drawer . . . little swords of wheat . . . fuzzy-hearted commas . . . a marimba of alchemy . . . canapés of flummery . . . my museum of desperate clues.* These poems stopped me in my tracks more than a few times. So moved by "A Swift and Fatal Plunge", I spent an evening reading about the tragic event that inspired Santer's stunning narrative. The notes I kept while reading *In Pearl Broth* will surely serve to inspire my own poem-making."

-Susan F. Glassmeyer, *Invisible Fish;* 2018 Ohio Poet of the Year

In *Pearl Broth*, poet Rikki Santer twists language. She employs metaphor, rhyme and her own wit, "She Verbs now She Nouns," to describe a world that, if not fallen, is at least one in which its inhabitants feel displaced. In Santer's poetic world, we are instructed to "Forget where you are, where you've been, where you're going. / Your global position is diminishing fast." Ours, the poet informs us, is an "age of clickbaiting, news farming, filter bubbling, / deep faking, hive mind and post truth. . . ." Nevertheless, Santer is aware and makes her readers aware of what we have lost by giving way to the post truth world, which she so ably satirizes. In one of my favorite poems, "In the Company of Flowers," the poet walks us through "rhythmic notations / vertical riffs of / ancestral petals / tiny gourds on tender edge / of rattle. . . ." The poem inspires us to let her witty description of a floral installation absorb and even heal our "memories of loss or love . . ." What more can we ask of poetry?

-Doug Rutledge, PhD
The Allure of Grammar: The Glamour of Angie Estes's Poetry

In Pearl Broth:
Poems New & Selected

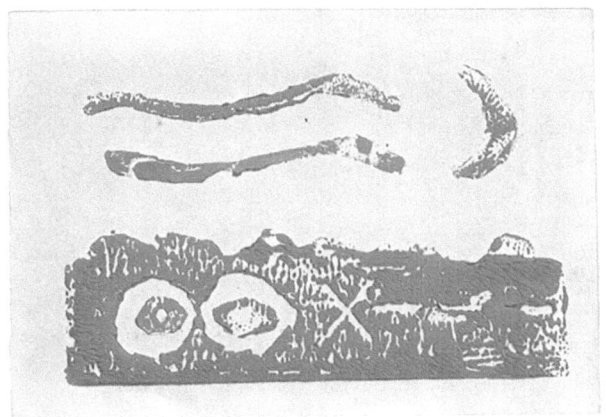

Poems by Rikki Santer

Stubborn Mule Press
Devil's Elbow, MO
stubbornmulepress.com

Copyright © Rikki Santer, 2019
First Edition 1 3 5 7 9 10 8 6 4 2
ISBN: 978-1-950380-28-2
LCCN: 2019939051

Design, edits and layout: Jason Ryberg
Cover artwork: Jon Lee Grafton
Title page image: Rikki Santer
All rights reserved. No part of this publication may be reproduced or transmitted in any form or by any means, electronic or mechanical, including photocopying, recording or by info retrieval system, without prior written permission from the author.

ACKNOWLEDGMENTS

My gratitude to the editors and staff of the following publications where the following new poems have appeared:

Plath Poetry Project: "Couriers"
Common Threads (OPA Anthology.): "The Heft of Wonder"
Poor Yorick: "Ginger Rogers Feathered Gown"
Erasure Showcase (Driftwood Press): "his post"
The Ekphrastic Review: "How to Cohabitant with a Kaleidoscope"
Cultural Weekly: "Launchpads," "Wig of the Bride of Frankenstein"
Chiron Review: "Parable"
Selah: "In the Company of Flowers"
Call Me [Brackets]: "While She Stands"
Driftwood Press: "The Business of Orange"
404 Ink: "Stephen Hawking Throws a Soiree for Time Travelers But This Time, They Show Up
Fifth Estate: "Curate This"
Ox Mag: "The Heft of Wonder"
The Comstock Review: "Bedroom Knocking at My Door"
Indolent Books/What Rough Beast: "Abracadabra Abecedarian"
Mojave River Review: "Is There a God Cento" "Now Playing: Everything I Said at the Party"
Gasconade Review: "Betty Boop Marries Herself"
Lumina: "Woman Painting Women" (and nominated for a 2019 Pushcart Prize)
Poetry Society of Tennessee (first place in Dr. Wanda Rider Memorial Award): "Leveler"

I am also grateful to the following publishers who believed in my work and strengthened it through their artful editing: Jason Ryberg (Stubborn Mule Press), John Burroughs (Crisis Chronicles Press), Dianne Borsenik (NightBallet Press), Sammy Greenspan (Kattywompus Press), Arthur W. Dawson (Kulupi Press) and the late Jennifer Bosveld (Pudding House) and to all my friends and colleagues in Salon and Bistro Poets, who shepherd drafts with wisdom and heart.

TABLE OF CONTENTS

I.

Betty Boop Marries Herself / 1
Betty Drops the Mic / 3
Betty Tosses Her Stilletos On
   My Bedroom Floor Again / 5
Dick & Jane, All Grown Up / 6
Star Virus / 9
Lunch with My Analyst / 10
RE: Secretaries From Hell / 11
What's With My Inner Zombie? / 12
Fairy Tale / 14
Garmin's Dr. Nightmare Speaks in Pantoum / 16
The Man of Ice Cream / 17
Blue / 18
The Business of Orange / 19
Bedroom Knocking at My Door / 20
While She Stands / 22
Couriers / 23
Midnight Wife Sleepwalking / 25
Wardrobe Conditional / 26
Parable / 27
Collectible / 28
Pedestrians in Between / 30
Under the Big Top / 31
Poem for Sin / 32
Museum of His Bumper Stickers / 33

Now Playing: Everything I Said at the Party / 34
Taxidermy for Erotica / 35
Curate This / 37
Leveler / 38
Abracadabra Abecedarian / 40

II.

Codifier / 42
Charles Darwin at the Beagle Point Mall / 45
Probabilities: An Inventory / 47
his post / 49
Deep As It Is Narrow / 51
When Sit Means Sit / 53
Follow Him / 55
A Swift and Fatal Plunge,
   And Then the Abyss of Sorrow / 58
Resharpening the Interim / 60
7th Son / 62
Depending on a Definition of What Is Is / 63
Stephen Hawking Throws a Soiree for Time Travelers
   But This Time, They Show Up / 64
Is There a God Cento / 66
You Can Call It / 68
The Heft of Wonder / 69
Villanelle Sonic / 71
In the Face of Another International Asteroid Day / 73

III.

Literary Movement: An Answer Key / 76
Spring Fashion Modeled by Rising Young Poets / 77
Baroness Elsa's Dinner Party / 78
Andy Warhol's Buffet of Thought... / 84
Arguments for Furniture / 85
Still Life with Whoopie Cushion / 88
John Cage Reconsiders Harmony / 89
This Space Reserved / 90
More Than They Should / 91
New Republic Princess / 92
Woman Painting Women / 93
How to Cohabitate with a Kaleidoscope / 96
In the Company of Flowers / 97
Launchpads / 98
Cinema Verite / 100
Double Feature / 101
Landscape Decrees / 111
Your Name Here / 113
Appetizers for Lunch / 115
Ginger Rogers' Feathered Gown / 116
Mon Oncle Aussi / 117
Wig of the Bride of Frankenstein / 118

All art is autobiographical. The pearl is the oyster's autobiography.

-Federico Fellini

always for Marc and Parker, my lifelines

I.

Betty Boop Marries Herself

Her camel kneels
& Betty steps down
into the midnight Ganges
feels the gentle push
of the current
when she submerges
the rose halo of
her linen robe tiptoes
into the swirls
and eddies
of the river's open
throat. Her voice
lightly bebops
the waters to sleep.
She feels the barge
of napping monkeys
make safe passage
from her *vagina
dentata.* Calla lily
behind her ear
she launches
into the darkness
a leaf bowl
filled with
frangipanis,

her carved love
spoon a confident
oar in the pearl
broth. Betty's curves
dissolve into the tender
pull of current, red
petals bobbing
to the surface
like a menstrual
milky way.

Betty Drops the Mic

In 1932, Helen Kane lost a $250,000 lawsuit against Max Fleischer and Paramount Publix Corporation for "exploiting her image." The defense brought out archival footage of Baby Esther, an African American entertainer of the late 1920s, known for her "baby" singing style.

Hiding behind the clothesline logic
of drying unmentionables
slung between fire escapes
& boarding house windows,

two faces emerge chafed
by scrubbing the stain
of done-me-wrong.
Our eternal vamp who

baited parades of imps
& urchins knew what
side her scaffolding was
buttered. Boop-boop-

a-doop, the vulgar epidemic
that became flesh of her flesh
& blurred the catechism
of appropriation. First, baby

voice thievery from Cotton
Club cabaret, then impotent
lawsuit for scat robbery.

The mouth of caricature sucked
on its own tired tail as Cab,
in the whitest of suits,
collected his paychecks.
Today Betty tilts her pink

pussy hat as she sashays
through her mounting stash
of shrink-wrapped &
unrepentant collectibles.

Betty Tosses Her Stilettos On My Bedroom Floor Again

Her autotune pokes me awake and 2:32 AM glares with its amber eyes. Koko's clown make-up caked in my palms and Bimbo snoring under my sighs. Betty's late late barhopping laces her neck like the fluttering arms of a goblin. She's the ampersand that won't leave me alone. Her stickers lick back at my tongue, her hairspray NutraSweet vexing the walls of my mouth. Betty lassoes me to her citizenship, most nights I'm her signature slot machine, brass fingers the throb in my gut. She gnaws on chocolate strawberries from my dizzy nightstand dish. OK OK I need me some sleep. *Get me crunked*, her mantra in black & white, my sheets licorice, my curtains cream. As Calloway twists his Hi-De-Ho libido, I shut my eyes but I'm still in her precinct, this time in Technicolor and Cinemascope—her emerald dress & orange bob. We shimmy inside a tiny holograph, call & response on merciless loop, baby talk in sound surround.

Dick & Jane, All Grown Up

Midtown Taxidermy is closed for remodeling. Too late
to pick up Spot. So with street parking and the promise
of linen table cloths, they duck into the bistro next door.
Mother's finally questioning Spam. Father's Edsel may be
impounded. The spines of their menus barely touch.
Dick arranges his radicchio; Jane breaks the bone of her
blackened steak. Did you get a call about the reunion
tour? Sally's liposuction left her loamy.

BROTHER DICK, salt & peppered bachelor, nursing
his appetite for half-baked scenarios,

squats beneath a yellowed kitchenette table
to answer a telephoned voice: *Angelique.*

Her tempo teases his quivering cheeks,
but he is remembering a shallow pool

of chocolate malted in his blender.
She coos a late night invite—erotic French

fry feedings—but his pattern is already
mapped, his last island always the kitchen.

The phone bell now cuts again
through the butter of his obsessions,

his jarring of all foods that come in loud boxes.
He knows it is her call. He climbs onto the stove

then curls fetal fashion to steal pilot heat, waiting
for the rings to stop. They stop. He sighs. He pierces

his cheek with a roasting thermometer—sliding
his eyes sideways to read. He's still undercooked.

*   *   *

SISTER JANE takes to fixing baked beans for breakfast, relishing
the smokey after-taste; a cowboy's mouth inside hers all during

rush hour. In her downtown cubicle, the warm sun on her back
is Earle's sun, too: massaging her through accounts receivable,

reviving him through cattle drives. For it was his diary she had
found— brittle and wedged between attic floorboards, giving

her reason to love stampede and the forgiveness he found in
cold night stars. She nuzzles against each browning phrase

which at any moment could crumble into the time that straddles
them. She jackdaws their life together into a bedside shrine;

velvet satchel for his words, acrylic frame for his fading
countenance—all her campfire's glow. She buys a Stetson, not his

hat at first, but night after night her scalp oils make it so: slightly oversized eases into perfection from caresses during

vacuumings and sitcoms. He seems not to object, enjoying the ride and the reincarnation, until the wedding dress

arrives—crisp, layered, and beaded—and the radio plays too loudly: *Your coffee's on the table but your sugar's out the door.*

Star Virus

Each thought experiment tumbles
through its own wormhole,

not reality, but the reality of exhaling
as a reality show star.

Cameras are the legislators
of ubiquitous grotesque:

abs cresting, boobs over-bloomed,
the corpulence of plenty to say.

Plato's shadow puppets in Dutch angle,
program makers casting with big bad

megaphones, choreographing
spectacles of Munchkinized shame.

Freak show as fable, landscapes
don't matter, citizenry that

gropes for kidney swaps, Z-list
celebrity, Sasquatch sightings

and one-way tickets to Mars.
To script or not to script, that

is the bloodstream. To hoax or
not to hoax, that is the delicacy.

Lunch with My Analyst

Give me just a taste of your paranoia, she directed. Not just the peas and carrots of elevator leers and sidewalk shoulder jabs but those steaming piles of *vienerschnitzel*—a knife point glistening midair, the metal aftertaste of arsenic in your ale. Locate that first moment when you bypassed battiness a la carte to fixate on entrees of overcooked delusion—scorpions climbing your skin, canaries cursing in Latin, all chased by one dopamine cocktail too many. Talk to me, she coaxed. Bare your soul and your prefrontal cortex. You're in good company. Franz and Vincent and Wolfgang are in the house, white gloved and waiting for their table.

RE: Secretaries from Hell

We are typing typing typing smuggling our words onto the backs of your furthermores and enclosed-you-will-finds. We draw fangs on the happy faces of your Post-It notes, stir powdered laxatives into your coffee creamers, hurl executive bathroom keys through the air vents of your waiting rooms. We will blame visiting children.

Some of us drive black '69 VW vans and like to curb our rusted fenders into your corporate parking spaces. We wear sunglasses at our desks and make secret lists of Naugahyde jokes. Often, we snicker at your matching teak veneer while lodging mint toothpicks into their pressboard frames.

We know where everything is. We have lunch beers and greasy hamburgers at Bruno's Rainbow Tavern. At pinball machines we dangle cigarettes from our rapid fire lips. We read Kafka in dark booths or sit with the other gals and talk about YOU.

We listen to Metallica tapes through our Dictaphones while balancing your ledgers. We alphabetize third world dictators into your Rolodexes. We nickname you boss a nova.

We perfect photocopied images of our hangnails, butts and bunions then send them to your clients in their SASE's. We submit your home addresses to occult mailing houses. We add categories to your While-You-Were-Out messages:
   ___Sounded Canine
   ___Missing Brain Matter
   ___Out To Get You, Too.

What's With My Inner Zombie?

Here
        emerging from my tent
of missing links
        wearing ellipses like
a pearl choker
        bedeviled
by paradoxes lurking
        in my temporal lode
by phrases I glee
        to the guillotine. I am
top heavy with the misleading architecture
        of mercy like when I'd put them
in baggies and drive over them
        with my jacked up Chevy when they
contracted dropsy each flapping goldfish body
        popping like a spore in a plastic
bubble sheet. Here
        setting the corner lot on fire
composting epic disasters with
        tainted brush strokes of insomnia
wriggling rascally earthworms in my teeth
        and rivulets of tar on my tongue.
Piffling questions multiply like maggots
        scurrying through the Etch a Sketch
of my mind, atop the skyscrapers in my pockets
        they amplify like a basket of tiny demons

tapping their way out of a baker's dozen of flaming
        eggs. I feel sticky, a bare legged Goldilocks
in a Lazy Boy gallery of toothy Naugahyde, riddle
        of ions in my brain's specks of jelly,
wispy wisps of protoplasm. I can't even.

Fairy Tale

Of all the baubles in her armoire, it was the tar
blossom brooch that pricked her sanity.

Sticky on her Abyssinian collar, it perched
selfishly, lured tendrils like a magnet.

Pooling stray coins, her stepmother,
stepsisters, mother-in-law had obliged

the traveling junk dealer when he knocked
on the doors of their resentment.

So she wore the trinket for her father
and husband, harmony's lie.

Until one day the archetype hardened
into the deepest black it could.

The snap crackle of its shell broke her
stepmother, mother-in-law, stepsisters

from their snoring, caused the town's
Richter scale to sit up and prattle.

Our princess went to her armoire
to find a pearl amidst her collar of balding

Abyssinian and when she wrapped it
around her tentative neck, she inhaled

a menthol of fresh iridescence
as her cellphone spawned a school of teeth.

Garmin's Dr. Nightmare Speaks in Pantoum

Speed it up, your global position is shrinking.
Take a swing by that bone yard if you will.
Cat tails and bat wings—it's time for some shopping.
Straight ahead until you see a ghoul in your mirror.

Take a right at the tattooed sphinx under a tattered umbrella.
Time and place could be loitering beneath the next billboard.
Head straight for that hitchhiking Waldo, bloody and bruised
Never mind that noise coming from your trunk.

Time and place now loiters in that billboard's teeth.
Your SUV is nice but it ain't no hearse.
Never mind the noise coming from the drunk.
Forget where you are, where you've been, where you're going.

This SUV got quite muddy so it's starting to curse.
Cat tails and bat wings—finally time for some gnawing.
Forget where you are, where you've been, where you're going.
Your global position is diminishing fast.

The Man of Ice-Cream

Ice me silly
he whispered
between stops
when the merry tingle
of his siren song
serenaded little tongues
slurping for his fingertips
while my groin churned.

Cream away the brine
of my impeached heart
I purred, as this hokey
pokey man twirled
his shimmering
rockets and greedy
bars from his silvery
emperor's box.

Truck me willy-nilly
as we winked
on cue and rounded
that last street
of his route
of our lust
of our soft
serve, desperate
and tainted.

Blue

Confessing right now will likely narrow my culinary latitudes but
I have decided hereafter to consume only blue which retrieves

no response from our kitchen window cerulean with moonbeams
as we crosstalk in ultra shades of just below red and just beyond

blue while the moonlight seems even noisier as it brushes across
a porcelain dish of sugar-dusted blueberries and a leftover mash

of Adirondack potato from our too late supper when you frowned
at your navel brimming with my angora fuzz harvested from that

aqua bunny hiding in its storybook cloud and you told me
that your appetite was too wet from all my self of steam but

I didn't mean to bait you or maybe I did with baskets of edible
blue pansies that our handsome new neighbor delivered this

morning in reversal of new-neighbor-welcome so now we both
feel harpooned like a pair of floundering lingcods with our flesh

that bright turquoise before we get cooked and my offer to stir
up our favorite nightcap of Grand Marnier and blue curaçao

is answered by two bottles that slip-shatter onto the blue-veined
marble and my mouth ringed with clown blue frosting and yes

> I guess
> I could have
> said less

The Business of Orange

was my mother's leather jacket, bold tangerine her private
blood pulse for arming a closet with the triumph of hue.

Now from her protege of color, my front door will command
you like a marmalade portal to a Pantone universe. My life

raft, a love for composites—juicy chemistry of saffron and
tomato saucing up my draperies and rugs. The divine rhythms

of infrared frequencies to harmonize with skies azure—and
mother sang, *smiling at me*. My father's protective tutelage

at the fruit stand—how to properly read the rind and dodge acid
headed for the eyes. A sudden bloom on my brother's city sidewalk,

umbrellas bursting open pumpkin and blue. Yet my Cara Cara
trees never survived Ohio, year-round sunlight temperamental

at best, but when my husband late at night brings me tea laced with
orange blossom honey, white petals softly light upon my breasts.

Bedroom Knocking at My Door

Like Mona Lisa's eyebrows fading
away like water on stone, my distant
bedroom from childhood returned
for weeks as memory's sine-waves
swerved like light from a star.

The gloss & sheen of morning's blue
hour, Broyhill back wall dresser, desk,
hutch, mirror, & one more dresser lined up
beneath the windowed brows of ceiling,
ivory creatures with heather trim &
a canopy bed with a bramble bonnet
of pink & white gingham where
swans would nest to cradle booklight
fantasies, marvelous dreams.

Mother, how you milled & conjured
the curves & edges of heartwood
to realize a daughter as the moon
organizes water. My ivy sky-wire
wallpaper, the ladders you planted
in my attitude, the caramels we chewed
a capella while swaying cross-legged
on the floor.

Confounding variables: You boarded
the slow train for multiple sclerosis.
Your pearls to be my pearls, stolen
from your nursing home safe. The broth
of your emptiness when father died
& I lived too many states away.

Last week I lost
one of the cobalt blue gloves
you bought me decades ago,
like a thief it secretly
slipped from my coat pocket
& next night next
nights that bedroom conducted its haunting:
your life-time achievement
for production design precision
& the daughter who will carry it
until she dies.

While She Stands

While she stands on the roof, *thud* pleads with her for consideration.
While she stands on the roof, salvation tries to nudge her from the edge.
While she stands on the roof, a pigeon overhead punctuates her
    shoulder for the soliloquy that ends with *Who cares?*
While she stands on the roof, the finger of a small girl from the
    window next door points at her, then draws circles in the air.
While she stands on the roof, she rewinds the scene with a spotlight
    beam streaming from dark clouds above.
While she stands on the roof, an umbrella laughs upwards twirling
    its colors amidst the legion of black ones far as she can see.
While she stands on the roof she measures each of her heartbeats
    & envies the sun that commits every morning to show up.
While she stands on the roof, her rumbling cell phone calls too much
    attention to itself, then is launched to the dumpster below.
While she stands on the roof, she is convinced she can fly, and
    for a few moments, she does.

Couriers

after Sylvia Plath

All I want right now are two
marshmallows and a nap

or the arcing neck of an eclair
swan. My mother's lullabies

dust down from the ceiling fan
onto my shoulders. In my weary

foyer I see room for everybody
ample as her front stoop. Moonlight

casts hulking shadows and
the hall mirror shows I'm just

another face on Mars with sneakers
under a robe. On the table this metal

thing's another countenance that's
got me tessellated by the throat,

my resting expression too stick-figured,
and thin thought, thin thoughts curl

around me like the tails of seahorses,
a tale that's drunk on petite shiraz

which tastes too philosophical for
its own good—over my head and

it's done, my magpie mind backmasking
a stairway to heaven for a riot of phantom

vows, losing my luster, my mooring.
Outside the picture window a choir

of inkblot callouses that snicker from
the front yard trees. Lies, lies my season.

Midnight Wife Sleepwalking

Deep in the dark belly of our backyard ravine
        I curl my tail over my nakedness and bury

my name under a congress of dead leaves.
        My bite settles for the tip of my tongue. I trot

ahead of myself through the birches, stop
        at the edge of giddyup, pass through it as

it passes through me. I roll onto
        a cardinal's remains that feather

my mane. Distant from two-legged
        upstairs snoring I am sway-backed

and hesitant as I compete for forest
        bandwidth—fellow supplicants in trill
& snort, spending the butter of pulse.

Wardrobe Conditional

It would have been smoother
if I hadn't been hijacked by his hat menagerie
crumpled against the circular wall
of a mildewed hat box, faded stripes
in hoarse harmony with themselves, or the
two I had taken from that sack
of discarded neckties left on the freeway's
meridian, three sixes swirled into the flavors
on each of its tongues.

If I could only rewind and unsee
the hawk's crime as it raided the murder
of crows, the limp blackness dragged
across the manicured lawn, the deconstructed
cloak of white down and black feather forsaken
while the helpless opera of grating caws
lingered like ghosts in twilight, or if only
I could reweave the peach and cream
gingham of a ripped party dress and erase
the red palm print stinging a six-year-old's thigh.

Parable

I instantly adored her. She knew her eggs,
delicate Faberge thrones atop her dresser,

buttery omelets glistening in her cast-iron pan.
After she learned I favored pencils—a basket

of eraser eggs delivered rainbow to my
doorstep next day. Then the kiss, platitudes

deep & sulfured that double-yoked me &
the calla lily placed between my breasts.

Our week scrambled on—the vamp of her
crotch, the boozy covenant of our sex,

slippery talk at Skully's, matching turtlenecks
& then me Monday morning bird-brained

and blister-packed having missed the velvet
tipping point for egg carton empty.

Collectible

Faded & stained was the last postcard he sent.
Through the stripes of coffee on a fuzzy ball

shore, tall grasses posed claiming for the camera
their susurrus while gulls flew upside down

& boulders were chia pets carpeted
in dayglow green. His message

blurred like Frost's voices
beyond a door, something about

a wizard he met teetering atop
a canoe docked in radioactive slime

who had said he'd be backstroking soon
to another planet. I filed this postcard

along with the hundreds of others
in a shoebox that once held stilettos

that my ankles had rebuked & now
it is my museum of desperate clues

from his expeditions to places
midwifed by his imagination &

straddling what was his reach
as well as his represented.

Through these postmarked images,
especially the calm precision of his

crosshair circles detailing the boutonniere
of a mime walking a tightrope, a rhyming

girl laughing in a funeral crowd, or a
hieroglyphic smear of blood reclining

across a bleached brick wall, he was branded
by the serious nonsense of his words that

expected long delays for the fastest way
out of town & strangeified the reverie of

what lived right up to the edges of
his moments that deftly dreamt mine.

Pedestrians In Between

Halfway between fur and feather
when instinct is the only imperative,

you'll wade through morsels of dew,
ramble down narrow paths, recognize

blue whispers from my hardscrabble
heart. Look for me in the charred ivory

of your dreams, see me slouching
into the paralyzed mist of a smoke

bush, chewing on rabbles of kudzu,
crabgrass, chickweed, thistle.

Two framed photographs survive
my desk: Gertrude pondering her stuffed

bookshelves behind her: a snapshot
of my little red wagon, its carcass rusty

and lost under a weeping willow's arms.
Sit with me one last time on this broken

bench in a backyard ravine and read
aloud the shadow calligraphy of a twisted

elm. Flecks of dark chocolate and
weary eyelashes will curate at our feet.

Under the Big Top

You speak to me at exactly
the wrong time but embedded
into the lining of your mouth
is exactly the right time
to name call with your most
slippery of knives.
I'm bolted insular into another
station of the cross, wobble
at juggling your steel
ball syllables. Where
is justice in the ambiguous
border of our circus
center ring? For Chrissake
look out for splinters,
blue sequined teardrops
on our prideful cheeks.

Poem for Sin

In line at the grocery she slaps her toddler for reaching, the wrapper bright red for envy at its point of purchase and I am in a vacuum looking away into my cart swaying with tuna cans for later when the calico's nose will nudge again again my sleeping palm while I dream of a blade at my landlord's wrist, then the twist of sloth snoring me hours past job after my thigh twinned with yours, luscious in the heat of hotel room, shy beast for enjambment of Venetian blinds and the psalms of sigh, thighs breaded with lust launching us high from their roots where muscles dissolve and dangerous vowels oblige again again.

Museum of His Bumper Stickers

Worship me. Let me count the ways.
I break for no one.
That's right. I killed joy.
Powerful wizards have the right to be judgmental.
Cock My Doodle Doo.
I'm not your daddy issue.
Swagger is my dagger.
I'm a semen fire hose.
If you can read this, back away.
Live studio audience down my pants.
I penis therefore I am.
Sarcasm: My breakfast of champions.
I don't do sorry.
For my next trick I will pull a bag of magic beans out of my ass.
My toys, my toys, my toys.
I'm master at pretending to care.
Honk if you finally see it my way.
Warning: You are in my blind spot.

Now Playing: Everything I Said At The Party

In the first hour I was full of flourish,
an almond tree tossing tender blossoms
to each co-worker, even to Sheila who
bogarts spotlight like a delinquent.
Then the jello shots played a glissando
& my history was erased with each
whisper-thin curl of my cigarette as irritation
ignored her Miranda rights. Was the zit
on Marlon's nose a barnacle named
Cro-Magnon, or Tina's Instragram
cat photos as stimulating as the mold
in my shower? Did Ruby's arugula salad taste
like fortified E. coli & Tim's EDM mix make me
want to drown myself in a biblical healing pool?
Did Bryce agree that her chronic nail biting was a
manual art most delectable & that her cousin's
cosseted life persists like a high-def hunk of throat-
gagging fudge? Into my morning coffee, sugar cubes
cannonball & this sound track sputters and skips.
My iPhone nuzzles under a pillow for shelter while
enemy machetes glisten in the social media of day.

Taxidermy for Erotica

Pose it under a glass dome,
a crown of cashew stems

sweet for the plucking.
How to recalibrate

those very first times
with frames around

the frames around
fifty shades of sway:

when a fig leaf curled,
when sex acquired a face,

when the antics of the gods
were painted naked.

Skin and stuff those dog-
eared novels fringed

with coupon bookmarks
and stained with parables.

Mount each cliché so high
it can't be reached:

buttered buttocks,
breast pyramids,

and pulpy organs
brimming with tiny

fireflies. There are no
second-rate motifs:

ravished claws
of the tigress,

lollipop groins and
ladies of the house

arching at supper
like porn stars.

Your clients cross and
uncross their legs

in pleasure of your bordello
handiwork: the primal

and the mechanical
swell and spread

into the timeless
marketry of exotica.

Curate This

> *How dreary — to be — Somebody!*
> *How public — like a Frog —*
> *To tell one's name — the livelong June —*
> *To an admiring bog!*
>
> — Emily Dickinson

Dogwoods swathed in delicate white, gently clear
their winter throats as cable news updates crawl and
grovel for her attention. But she doesn't blog, pin, Snapchat,
Instagram or—GodNo!—tweet, and her dumb phone's
shortcomings are just fine. She the freak in the waiting
room without an umbilical glow in her palm, just
a paperback copy of something she fills with marginalia.
Too many frogs posting and posting and posting
for nods from bogs brimming with hyper-focused
somebodies, while apps like tight-assed pimps,
book faces and fingerprints for everlasting control.
The globe churns away with liars, trolls, and vampires
who favor their weapons virtual then visceral
but what else is new except now they pontificate
and pulverize at digitized speeds.
In this age of clickbaiting, news farming, filter bubbling,
deep faking, hive mind, and post-truth,
a tsunami brews for our collective reckoning.
Footage won't save us from the ruptured corners
of an asylum imploded—the Mob of Me stranded
waist deep and wedged tight.

Leveler

after *Toilets of the World* by Morna E. Gregory and Sian James

Bowing to the deities of bodily function
        and the privilege of solitary relief
with push, pull, twist, crank, flush or stomp
        we all discard that which comes forth.

In crescent moonlight of a Tennessee outhouse
        or before a frescoed urinal in a Wisconsin museum.
In Hong Kong's 14 karat gold bathroom
        or l'urinette in Montreal's Whiskey Cafe.

Back-lit glass walls in Johannesburg's Kilimanjaro Nightclub,
        London's pop-up urinal rising from its manhole cover
like a god. From the trunk of a dried cactus in Bolivia's salt desert,
        under a weathered handprinted *bano* sign

where scant pesos are collected for a family's basic needs.
        Count your rubles for a public loo in Moscow,
spend thin air at a stone commode, stoic in the High Andes.
        In Germany or France, a *klofrau* or *madame pipi* may

assist you; Japan could pamper you with heated seats, water jets,
        then dryers to blow you clean. Double billings of *weewee*
or *doodoo* flushes, curry-scented pink tents or a campfire's
        nearby pee tree. Crouch over a hole with two footprints

like porcelain quotation marks, aim at dodging fish or
    painted bees. Australia's dunnies & longdrops inventoried
for a National Toilet Map. Iceland's no-squatting-man signs for
    cemeteries at the mercy of tourists rudely carefree.

Shallow indents by the side of dirt roads, or on ocean lips
    impoverished rows of rickety huts on stilts—
our toilets tell their tales of us,
    & our drowsy tolerance that disregards full

global access to running water on a planet
    spoiling with dysentery & cholera
until nature calls us   all
    to our knees.

Abracadabra Abecedarian

Archetype of these times, the theater swathed in inky
black velvet, the gyre of dwelling in the prestidigital age,
cat & mouse of it, gallery of creased brows that lend virtuosity in
deviance with each deal, no end to
enthrall to mesmerism, just feast on the
fusillade of his growling tweets, firehose of a flame that just
    can't clear its
goosenecked throat & leaves us
handcuffed like Houdini; how to expose that formula of
invisibility when illusionists try to get as much as possible from a
jackdaw of props; he thinks he is the King Kong of cards,
knowing how the trick is done but not how to do it,
levitating the taproot of daily news;
mirrors ripple in their angles of incidence,
newsfeed seance, stage doors first slightly propped
open, then gummed shut, as he
palms the next head floating; the dove from his top hat
quacking partisan facts wrinkled & rough &
ready to rise from his teetering
sarcophagus, each syllable rumbling MAGA MAGA MAGA, his
trick with a title that's
utterly realistic but not real & could
vanish like the smoke puff of tenuous success so we
watch like an audience who yearns to believe in a good witch not a
xenophobic witch of the west & we turn the channel, the cheek
    & struggle to loosen the
yoke of media obsession & pray that when our sight lines finally
zigzag across stage, they'll settle on an empty cabinet where the
    elephant has vanished.

II.

Codifier

for Annie Jump Cannon (1863-1941), American astronomer whose cataloging work was instrumental in the development of contemporary stellar classification.

You strained
to hear
the teacup

clatter, the pink
chatter while
spectral dust

glistened
in your
ears.

Valedictorian
tethered to
itemizing

the heat and
cold of stellar
fingerprints,

census taker
of the flaring
up, caving in,

and going out.
Star light, star
bright by candle

light atop
your childhood
roof you basked

in the *sort of*
and *as if,*
counting

constellations
thatched on
their velvet grid

of indifference.
Then Wellesley
Radcliffe, Harvard

to nurse your
spectrographs,
your dense flocks

of stars—400,000,
a lifetime's
tally. Orion

deep and wide,
spiral arms
of galaxies,

supernova
remnants—
you relished

their rewind
of time.
Your life's

orbit not as
effervescent
as it could be

but still
you perched,
devotee

on tiptoes
to launch
from your

threshold
to become
a *fine girl kissed*

over and over
by the quenched
lips of history.

Charles Darwin Visits the Beagle Point Mall

This ship of concrete and steel entices.
With his leather journal in hand, his icon
of a beard points the way through a vaulted

entrance fit for a Victorian queen. Darwin's
notations are quick like snake tongues: misplaced
sea gulls churn the winter sky, salt-laced

hordes of vehicles grid a sloshy inlet.
How the awful scope of his idea
has thrived in this moonscape of terrazzo,

neon, and brass. Darwin's finches roost in the rafters
of a glass sky which pronounces heaven down upon
its colonies—curious clusters that frolic in shallow pools

of noisy marketry. He notes the arpeggio of species,
the dance of the bread and circus: Mothers with
puffy strollers scuttle across watery marble;

hooded teenagers with spiny legs and droopy
plumage swagger like blue-footed boobies,
and the sea lions—so many sea lions of varying madriffs.

Kiosks are archipelagoes that nurture treasures:
Godiva oysters, mineral make-up, doll babies
more angelic than angels. The mall tilts on its axis.

Toddlers slip atop a herd of fiberglass tortoises;
Roaches scurry across the deck of a food court.
Suddenly Darwin is feeling seasick from the sugary

waves of scents and too many squealing eddies
of chatter. So he dons a pair of shutter shades from
the Spy Eye Shack and finds refuge in the folds

of a deep couch. In this demo room, he likes pondering
his countenance as it multiplies across a bank of high
definition TVs, each saturating color like the devil.

Probabilities: An Inventory

Footprint in a slab of stone,
the flattest moment of a sea,
a rook blindsides a queen, &
cigarette smoke stuttering
in 80% chance of rain.

Secret bag of caramels in a lingerie drawer,
a postcard surprises with fractal confessions,
white lies lurk in the cavalier folds of promise,
the melody of a hyphen to uncommon degrees.

The way in is filament
for the way out:
fingers at attention in my rock paper scissors holster,
my fist rubbernecking knee deep in algorithms:
vindictive scissors.

Waiter, make my thinking malted,
a layer cake of spider webs made spicy
with the stuff of the world—
the nervous matter of my mind
seeking anchorage in the evening
& morning wardrobes of Venus.

The way out weighs in again:
venture into the pyrotechnics
of another thunderstorm
for the next parade
of lottery numbers
from the neighborhood
convenience store, shoreline between
predictable barbs of fragment.

his post

redacted from Walt Whitman's "This Compost"

1

                      I thought I was safe

                                      to meet my lover

O how can it be

      every

               generation

      deceiv'd

                    press
               it
             foul

2

Behold

The bean bursts noiselessly through the mould

    e rection of the wheat   out
          of graves

    he-birds

                 break through

                         strata of sour

That it is safe to allow it to lick
              with its tongues,
That all is clean forever and forever,
                        tastes so good,
                           juicy,

  when I recline
          every spear   rises out of what was
      once a catching disease.

 such sweet things
 harmless and stainless

     exquisite winds

             accept
             at last.

Deep As It Is Narrow
after Ricky Jay on Matthias Buchinger (1674-1740)

Tonight, in the elbow between segments of sleep,
armed with magnifying glass, I zigzag in wonder
with a modern day magician and his 18th-century
companion: Matthias, *The Little Man of Nuremberg*
who was s master of micrography, born without hands
or feet, a 29-inch-tall overachiever, little more
than a trunk of a man who cut quills
with finlike stumps and a knob of flesh
to write upside-down, right-side-up,
backwards, and forwards the tiniest of tiny
Biblical psalms that secretly meandered
in iron gall ink through portraiture hair
curls or laced the Lord's Prayer
within the diameter of a shilling all
which caused me to remember
in sixth grade when I filled pages and pages
of spiral-bound notebooks with dense tracks
of W's, all those penciled burrows multiplying
escape from school's confinement: rounded
for Pip's ever so many partings, pointed
for thick tangles of angled axioms, barbed
for monotoned defenses of Manifest Destiny
and it was W, my father's invented middle initial
engraved into his battered briefcase, and
W, my private cartography for descending

into caverns of wonder, so tonight
as I retrieve from a drawer that which is poised
in archival sleeves, my father's steady
penmanship curls sweetness
into long distance letters
but also tight-fists of between
the lines narrow for an illegitimate
sibling he erased for me.

When Sit Means Sit

Don't placate me
with cushiony
vowels or
sugar the treat
in treatment.
I want
to be strap
happy without
bucket bags
of sea salt
at my hips.
Deflated beach
balls carpet
my knees and
I've learned how
to recede elegantly
after the stranded
and forlorned.
I sit on runways,
in meridians,
with memories
that park on
their haunches—
Velcroed to Graviton
when the floor
drops and my summer
tube top starts

creeping down,
your tighty-whities
and the swaying
of your ribs, sadness
your only posture
at the table.
I'm seated,
ceded
on the throne
of early morning
dreams that jump
cut me through
the traffic
of anxiety.
To gaze then graze
with a book
in my lap,
the beneficent
faith of easy
chair—levitating
above a sea
of white petaled
confetti from
my backyard pear tree
glossy eggs
in the wren's nest cup
the soft tug
of a guide dog,
guide god.

Follow Him
for Stephen Bishop (1821-1857),
lead explorer and guide to Kentucky's Mammoth Cave

Antebellum paradox. The mixing
of bloods didn't free you but
your subterranean prowess

gave you momentary relief.
If you could, would you burst
through the milky membrane

of history like the showman
you were to claim the libretto of
your life: puppeteer and puppet.

Slave with a lantern, sweet talker
with harmony on your tongue--
the bitterness of the South,

and the honey dream of Liberia.
They followed you in your slouch
hat, the white elite in their long

skirts, starched shirts, through a
bonanza of labyrinths—no neat
set of steps but corkscrew paths

of sideshow thrills. They followed
you trying the dark and your blood
paths. Tapestries of sound—your call

and response in echo chambers,
your gospel sing-alongs floating
atop underground rivers, then

salvation in midnight grace notes
whispered moist in your Charlotte's
ear. Keen as those eyeless fish

your stealthy handholds traversed
unknown depths and keyhole orifices
like Kafka in his burrow. The miles

and miles of connected veins you
sketched from memory, topography
stitched through your bones. Your

bold byline when published, but
Master reaped the royalties and
altered your place names to suit

his own. Screech owl your turntable,
wrens scat copacetic and generations
still follow you. Union soldier's tomb

stone repurposed for you years
later as a moon-eyed afterthought
like the soot-etched autographs

you left on damp cave walls
marking the theater of your
inheritance, of your cage.

*A Swift and Fatal Plunge, And Then the Abyss of Sorrow**

for Dodo Kumaritashvili, mother of Nodar , the 21-year-old luge athlete who died in a training run at the 2010 Vancouver Olympics

Each week, with stones brimming from
her dress and coat pockets, she trudges

up and down the Trialeti mountains
in a dense progression of switchbacks.

Her small granddaughter nourishes her
enough to return home to a silent

kitchen where she prepares the stroganoff,
goulash, and herring that he loved.

Those evenings, she arranges the meal
for him atop his bedroom desk, then

sits for a while among the trophies,
photographs, and posters. Hours lapse

and then she clears the delicacies to
deliver them to neighbors or passing

strangers. Sleep rarely can loosen
the grip of that fatal 270-degree turn.

In the middle of restless nights she wanders
outside into the freezing darkness not

stopping for shoes or coat. *I was just going
to walk until I died.* She rewinds his final

moments, stretches next to him in that last
sled and peers through the racing space

between his feet to watch the smooth
and icy umbilical cord of track unfurl.

Behind the church, through flimsy wire fencing,
pigs and cattle plod over his grave. *Not even*

one percent remains, she says
of a woman that was.

*headline from *The New York Times*, 2/1/14

Resharpening the Interim

Pencils should be better
privileged, their gift
of starting over.

So many working titles--
some of us envy others,
others don't mind

on the sly,
on the run,
most ache to trust

tenderness, lust for
more days insatiable
with *nomnomnom* color.

To speed up that feedback
loop for more toys to hitch
to a star, logrolling so fast

in our own cartoons.
But it's all in pencil
as we compress towards

the gray horizon. Slow
down from the rewind--
sketch the last face

that will say I love you,
your last day to erase
the slate clean.

7th Son

for Anthony Bourdain

no Frank O'Hara hail this summer's morning
but still it hit me hard on my head the headline
your suicide in France   hungry
ghosts hammered jabbed & tatted you
stoic bad boy joy certain
of nothing   raw journey's
last bite   blue chrysanthemum at last
unperturbed

Depending On a Definition of What Is Is

Trolling for the Master Bait?
Each ontological bon-bon so creamy

in the middle, a perfect aftertaste for gazing
at outey or iney, which renders us breathless

with its fuzz or crepe. With leather and ladders
strapped to our backs, we like handcuffing

matters down. To get a grip on that orgasmic
dictum that can turn on the most virgin

of skeptics. All syllogisms curl their toes,
especially when a glossy centerfold opens

onto a paradigm posing. The meaning
of meaning lusts after this:

Dollops keep dolloping.
Bed springs just spring.

Stephen Hawking Throws a Soiree for Time Travelers But This Time, They Show Up

First the professor coordinates space and time—
52 degrees, 12 minutes, 21 seconds north
0 degrees, 7 minutes, 4.7 seconds east—
another sumptuous recipe from geography,
which easily rivals sliced bread.
On the counter, his Foodini printer gleams ready
for any 3D Frankenpastry that may be desired.
As time breaks its moorings, Simpson cartoon
clouds part and light seeps into full moon.
Worm-holed planks of a buffet table snap into place,
bouquets of jewel-toned balloons punctuate the drawing room
then in response to the muscular lilt of his grin
doors of an interplanetary elevator open
and his guests, having crossed borders
through a gizzard squeeze, leave snail
trails on the silk brocade while packing
deus ex machina in their pockets.

Hawking's pendulum clock, steady and sure,
ticks out a town for these tourists—
togas and tuxedos, low-backed dresses
and black turtlenecks, silver spandex,
and light-weight spacesuits bio-engineered.

They sample canapés of flummery
topped with quantum foam,
five loaves and two fishes,
a platter of forbidden fruit,
a 12-tiered cake studded
with Marie Antoinette's pearls,
Cleopatra's stuffed pigeons,
Vitellius's flamingo tongues,
armadillo fricassee especially
for Darwin, breakfast eggs
with porcini mushrooms
if Einstein decides
to sleep over.

As each moment buds into another,
a troupe of grandfathers and grandmothers
wield paradox shields
as they linger and swell
around a holographic sundial.
And over there H.G. raising
a Waterford flute of champagne,
steadies a nod to Stephen
with his mustache.

Is There a God Cento

We were on Tibetan translucent time
The once the now the then and again.

As you would eat the fingertips of god,
dress lifted off a mannequin to reveal nothing.

The hard darkness is padlocked with a huge heart,
no place to put a key or lock or unlock.
So you invest
authority in signs
you cannot read with any accuracy.

Which train are we on
is there a quiet car
is there a car for weepers
the tic of prayer persists in nonbelievers.

You can't have god in with the luggage.
As it happened I drowned the ants
on the plate to stop being God to them.

The waiting room was bright
and too hot. It was sliding
beneath a big black wave,
another, and another.
Like thoughts, some become monuments.

And the circus tent with its acrobats, stern-faced
and gilded, circling the ring on their parallel horses.
Act so that there is no use in a centre.

Gratitude to the following poets: Anne Waldman, C.D. Wright, Ales Steger, Sam Sax, Lynn Emanuel, Louise Gluck, Alicia Suskin Ostriker, Alice Fulton, Roy Bentley, Carol Snow, Elizabeth Bishop, Linda Bierds, Gertrude Stein.

You Could Call It

You could call it ● Little Circumstance ● because of its shortitude ● and wide shoulders ● that circle back to the comedians ● inside your thought balloons. ● It all ties together ● like the Beelzebub ● between the belly laugh and the belly cry ● like Thoreau's *hush* and *whoa* ● like the chieftains in your very own banana-peeled universe. ● You could call it ● Shadow Boxing ● a palimpsest from central casting ● Marlene Dietrich's gorilla suit gone sticky ● from the paws of critique dogs ● their dogma gnawing on greased lightning. ● You could call it ● once for dinner ● twice for keeps ● a tenant hot-plating it in an illegal warehouse ● the Clear and Present ● the Cupcake Resurrection ● Epiphany's Dive into the sunset. ● It could turn and call you out ● for your zoo tattoo ● for your backers who back themselves ● for your flummoxed votes ● your candy appled frequencies ● your surrender to the Cloud. ● So call it what you may ● and what you may not ● the never ● the ever ● that burrows into the quicksand of tropes ● and now almost extinct, the roundness of dialing.

The Heft of Wonder

How the blind boy in
the gallery tastes arm-

in-arm every painting
through her words.

Elementary school angels
with flat halos and cardboard

wings. Nicotine's momentary
pardon from crisis. The hopeful

pageantry of a going-out-of-business
sale. *America's Got Talent,* that lamb

of a girl who jettisons into a rock
& roll lion her boot tassels chiming.

How amber can time-travel
a prehistoric frog. The typeface

and font size of a snake's rattle.
A congregation of air bubbles

to corral krill for a hungry
team of humpback whales.

How flutterings italicize the fledging
on a steady branch. The throat

of a vagina that pines for love
and punchlines that can be trusted

like the measured weight
of a mother grizzly's paw.

Villanelle Sonic

Gravitational waves were detected on September 14, 2015 at 5:51 a.m.
Eastern Daylight Time by both of the twin Laser Interferometer
Gravitational-wave Observatory (LIGO) detectors, located in
Livingston, Alabama and Hanford, Washington, USA.
                              (www.ligocaltech.edu)

We strain to penetrate the silence
to hear waves reverberate through spacetime,
as Science lures supernova wildness

when black holes collide. They churn and chime to coalesce,
their din a history traveling eons in rhyme.
We strain to penetrate the silence

and imagine spectacular moan and chirp, decibels dense,
a billion trillion trillion watts scraping spacetime
as Science listens for a sound spectrum's guidance

with the purest of mirrors, stunning transparence,
a laser's shadow of events now sonic and divine.
We strain to penetrate the silence

with persistence to intercept light-years of resonance,
the ear, now more privileged than the eye,
as Science imbues its fresco of mathematical giants
for a soundtrack to accompany silent movies beyond the skies.

To hear waves in the curves of spacetime,
we strain to penetrate the silence as Science
coaxes cosmic whispers to reveal what may well be timeless.

In the Face of Another International Asteroid Day

The more we learn about asteroid impacts, the clearer it became that the human race has been living on borrowed time,

-astrophysicist Brian May, Ph.D.

This morning a bee in my car
made malady of my driving
but when on the side of the highway
that little worker finally escaped
it was the promise of honey.

Could we be next dinosaurs?
Siblings of Tunguska, Chelyabinsk?
How to barricade the keyhole
to an eccentric path of a monster
mountain from space?
Imagine a next chaos of brittle
dispatches from ashen lips
details of fever clouds, ragged
prayers for streets of tomorrows.

Islands of physicist-priests nurse
equations like finicky orchids
so I pass my finger safely
through a candle flame,

veer right for flashing sirens,
cherish distance from beheadings,
drive-bys, hungry Ebola, the fawn
that drowned last spring in the mud.

Tonight June moon
the satin pool
of a wedding dress
dressed in firefly
arpeggios launched
with mission
and abandon.

III.

Literary Movement: An Answer Key

1. Read, then rinse. Never vice versa.

2. The knife and fork of starlings usually volunteer.

3. Diary sketches that show what their lovers would do that summer without them.

4. It was unadvisable to wear flat hats. Their heads were suspicious of platters.

5. The saltiest statue; the shadow box most savory. Answers will vary.

6. Spun gold was served up in candy dishes with glass feet.

7. When Idea was blind, folded, hood winked.

8. Biography was neither puddle nor choke hold.

9. Roget's conch.

10. The dark gloss of future through a screen door.

Spring Fashion Modeled by Rising Young Poets
-0 (The Oprah Magazine)

Stock the shelves with shrink
wrapped metaphors. The Poetnistas
are here. Each pronounced a connoisseur,
cherry-picked from the stacks. Each packaged,
full-paged and ankle deep
in her very own reflecting pool.
What eight goddesses who write poems
are wearing.

She Verbs now She Nouns.
Their verses pervert into accessory, sink
into sand, stretch across a megaphoned
hard-on, are knifed and forked
on a porcelain plate. *Her zen minimal is*
channeled through the clean lines of
a French-cuffed shirt. The teal,
peach and chartreuse of a pencil
skirt and sequined cardigan make
her feel va-va-va voom.

Frame us, too, salacious
window lickers fit for a fitting
room where beatnik turtlenecks
and black toreador pants hang
whimpering on another clever hook
of commodity.

Baroness Elsa's Dinner Party

for Elsa von Freytag-Loringhoven (1874-1927),
avant-garde poet and first American Dadaist

From Elsa's wall, H.D. grabs a mirror on which she arranges
salamis and sugar doughnuts in Freudian procession.

>   Else:
>   What mystery is this?
>
>   You are Orpheus idealized,
>   female androgyne, art circle jewel.
>
>   Your long fingers poised,
>   lyre in repose, your days your art;
>
>   birches gleam their countenance,
>   poppy eyes at your feet.
>
>   You call forth nephrite and purple turmaline
>   from your Lechter, your rare bird.
>
>   Biddle summons your Hydra heads,
>   pound for pound you are Cassandra unleashed
>
>   rallying against cast iron lovers
>   wedged inside cannons.

> O Amazone incarnate, trolling
> this graveyard of *unburied shells of souls.*

Applause erupts. Edith Sitwell's cigar bobs in her lipsticked mouth. A lullaby for dada:

> AT THE vermilion cotillon
> She was the steeped European
> Madame Flaneur of this town
> Skyscrapers her crown.
>
> A most musical belle,
> Teaballs dangling from swells;
> Ice cream spoons scooping lobes,
> black lipsticked OÆs
>
> Oh oh oh oh
> *Heia! ja-*
> *Hoho!*
>
> Madame Flaneuse she trots
> Rubber tires, tired knots,
> dolls and soldiers on her hems,
> horse blanket pins in their pens.
>
> For sex she wickedly confesses
> Marcel, Carlos, avant-garde contessas.
> Inspired barking and larking,
> Paintings rearranged, shrills arcing

> Till the moon and marionettes sleep
> On tenement steps where cherubs weep
> The Baroness has left the shore
> Life mocked by Chance and core.

Laura Riding balances a plate of raw broccoli and dark chocolate on her knee caps and whispers into Elsa's ear, *the world and you.*

> The frame followed you across the sea.
> Brutality is and wills its way
> Until it is in each breath
> And breath wills it to be.
> Your gaiety rises but only against the sorrow
> That gives it the meaning
> You can't fully understand.
> So words and deeds become ghosts--
> And the brutality of the frame keeps them close
> Until fragments and segments compress and implode.

The peeling door is kicked open. Myrna Loy bounds into the flat; her scarves form a halo, a modern woman:

> A silver figure
> dances nude
> on mirrored sidewalks

Her feet are wheels
 - - - her jewels
utilitarian.

Miscellany
 and the forbidden
her luminous wands - - - -
body is her theater
her museum her notebook.

Without a country
the banner unfurls
against the chatty walls
of salons and blindman balls
while lampshades
monopolize moments
and

feathers are strewn.
Taillight conquers bustle ---
Cross dressing threatens kings.
A coded script to be deciphered
by many daughters who will follow
- - - -dauntless - - -
Evolving us - - - -

Gertrude Stein's palms are on the table tapping in beat with the hissing oil. Her fingers make hieroglyphics in the flour then raise a jelly jar of bourbon to Elsa's buttons:

AN UMBRELLA.

A spoke is one answer. Trajectory from any gutter makes charm. In corner, in center, in a frame that is this room all dark all light. *Why is there a difference between one window and another?*

A HAT.

Aviator's grin. Ears hear fears. Scuttle inverted to broach a vegetable grater. A shaved head declares the meaning of violet. Transformation knows into pose.

A HAT.

Carrots or beets are the haberdasher's commas.

HATS.

Rayman's frame. Halo web like a cage. Choker chokes tenderly.

A BOWL.

If purpose is chipped, *any where is crumb.* Yolk wins. Stamps tattooed are cereal flakes.

A SOUND.

Rat laps. Philosophical about scraps.

A SOUND.

Egg beater propelled by ears.

A CAGE.

Canary reasons and refutes. If the warrior is standing, if the selection is arranged, if the arrangement is not arranged in arrangement, if the color is fearless.

Andy's Warhol's Buffet of Thoughts at the Kahiki Supper Club

I'm feeling like a pu pu pu pu platter machine.
Here I am, the MSG of your party, your ambassador of kitsch.
All this South Seas camp is so deliciously saucy.
Bring me another steaming plate of quotation marks, please.
I adore this place…it's the Louvre of American irony.
I'm getting swept away by the eye-shadow-turquoise of the
    Mystery Girl.
But you need more Ken dolls at the Outrigger Bar.
The Scorpion, The Headhunter, The Coconut Kiss— they all
    make me want to live a la Polynésienne.
I could just tap dance atop one of those gongs while the gossipy
    tittle-tattle from that parrot seduces me.
Wrap your legs 'round a palm tree and I'll make a lodestar of you
    with my Polaroid.
Should I autograph your napkin— the tip of your tongue?
I suspect this lingering afterthought of Spicy Kung Pao Shrimp
    is Duchamp's doing.
Even these leftovers are Time Capsule-worthy.
I'll have more of the soup.

Arguments for Furniture

That first rock, first log
to support our repose
to hold up our world.

When is a chair not a chair?
When it's sentient, defiant,
protesting the amorphosized
foot, leg, arm.
No high back ideals here
just a need to serve,
to keep bodies off the ground.

How many chairs does it take
to heal the planet?
The laquerwork of promise,
the cantilever of belief.
Foyers connected
doorway by doorway
strung across the globe—
we are seated, waiting together.

Cradles for young Vikings,
seesaws for young at heart.
What is bruised, stained,
and broken
on a tree lawn.

What is leaning
on a dirt floor.
The cluttered landscape
of kitchen table
as I write this.

Behold the dictatorship
of the hand—
drawer rendered eunuch,
armoire defying gravity,
every stool a philosopher,
the moody horizons of bed.

Sit with iconic spells—
a painter's mother, war plans
negotiated in the round,
a golden girl's serried
samplings of porridge,
the ergonomics of psychosis
reclining, the electric last throne
for a killer.

Inventory the furniture zoo—
the most exquisitely
tensiled, tubular,
mortised, or mitered,
the rarest exemplar of line,
table with the deepest
identity complex,

cabinet with the best
sense of humor,
biggest bag of beans.

Furniture revives our sitter status
survives the timber of our days
and the rocker explains it all.

Still Life with Whoopie Cushion

It ain't lowly novelty for Madame who likes her money
straight up with all faces facing her, she the supreme curator
of cheap laff exotica. Behold her credenza draped in lustrous
black velvet, read her realm from left to right fixed
in one silenced moment of thigh-slapping theater. Fake fly
sprawled atop a Mortimer Snerd incisor, overbite sublime;
alabaster bust of Soupy Sales, rivulets of dried pie cream at his
neck round his bulging eyes. Sinews of Renaissance light
frame this hearth of tactical jokes that hold us in their spell.
Not a porcelain platter of purple figs dripping with juices,
but a crude heap of smashed trick fingers with assorted breaks
in their rubber skins just ripe for alarming; fat pitcher sweating
its cherry Kool-Aid grin with a dribble glass tipped
in mid-weep; whoopee cushion all ego all vanity, pink pearly,
viscuous flesh promising razzberry succulence. This still life
frames the language of monkeyshine. Not broken bread,
vacant oyster shells, or lemon rinds spiralling but the spillings
of Cachoo powder, fabric snakes spent and sprung from
peanut brittle cans, and a dappling of puddles glistening
plastic puke or doggie doo. Through the room's beveled
window, clouds hover wearing our voyeur moustaches,
tips twirling upwards Snidely Whiplash style.

John Cage Reconsiders Harmony

His head inside a temple bell tiny temple
        bells inside his head/he shapeshifts

into a zen galaxy of shimmering silence, tiptoes
        onto a sunlit spider strand swaying

with rhymes of dew drops. Listen. Ghost
        moans and mewing from the belly

of deep sea/primordial fungi in emerald
        songs from crystal goblets. Sip

color frequencies, the sweet persimmon
        of sacral chakra. As stopwatch

ticks and yarrow stalks mix, his footprints
        scribble scrabble over sands of

self and soul. The bark, the bray, the squeak,
        the thrum. No walls. No vessels.

No music. All music. All vowels and consonants
        seeping from Void.

This Space Reserved

> *The silence on the floor of my house is all*
> *the questions and all the answers that*
> *have been known in the world.* –Agnes Martin

Her parking space was threaded
with weeds, cross hairs through
concrete. Interlopers, we cupped
our hands around our eyes
to survey through milky
studio windows. Paintbrushes
numb and canvases paralytic,
the scene echoed an absent-
minded agenda that poked her
on her way.

Later museum docents tipped us
towards her apartment of assisted
living, the empty beach
of her wooden blinds,
more grids to murmur mystery.

There at her threshold
we were suspended,
teetering in the well
of her Tang Dynasty saucer.
Then clarity rained softly
and we left her undisturbed
to sip her last two months,
then ashes beneath
an apricot tree.

More Than They Should

> after *A Dangerous Woman: The Art of Honore Sharrer*
> Exhibit, Columbus Museum of Art; 2017

Sidesaddle on her gander and in voluptuous
nakedness, Mother Goose hovers above
the unrhyming of her rhymes.
Her canvases are trampolines for curveballs—
steady eyes from an army of nude
Ledas defiant against Rubenesque leers
and unhinged from all slithering swans.
Instead, they demand their posed universes
be picture-locked into liberating subversion—
chairs float, domestic pups screw, a slab
of raw meat prays for us all. An alphabet
of random knives, forks, and plates
punctuate the dangers served up in bold
platters of irony and the owls, those owls
that seem to know more than they should.

New Republic Princess

>for *Princess Victoire of Saxe-Coburg-Gotha*
>—Kehinde Wiley; Toledo Museum of Art

How to punctuate with a last painting
in his *New Republic Survey,* wall
after wall banquet of proud, haloed faces
that arrest us with commanding scale,
sensuality of full-bloomed skin,
simmering frames serving up dense
backgrounds that sauce, fire, nourish
each subject's reclaimed identity.

Behold this dessert of quiet grace,
Princess with her back turned to us.
Belted firm in wide copper with flow
of sheer forest green raiment, taut
mahogany shoulders, lush mountain
of ebony hair. Her tranquil confidence
fuses with a thick curtain of flower
and vine that entwines and courts her
as she surpasses her tepid lily-white
sister with a warm and ready
hand to take ours.

Woman Painting Women

*Let us not forget the horror that accompanies
the wonder; the horror of this story…*
    —Marie Darrieussecq *Being Here is Everything:*
    The Life of Paula Modersohn-Becker (1876-1907)

Those who recall me claimed
Paula puzzled Paula—
suspicious of childbirth, flirtatious
with a bell-tower's dangling rope,
impatient with cooking classes,
miserable veal roast.

Copper kettle of long thick hair,
my commanding gait
through the moorlands of Worpswede.
My painter husband rubbed pristine
bark and leaves between his fingers.
I, with chalk and charcoal, limned
dignity into what was gnarled—
peasants bound to the soil
sunken women weathered
and work-worn, their thick
hands like spades, tidy
mouths in tangles of thought—
and little girls forever sequestered
from womanhood

but pensive just the same—
my sisterhood in foxgloves,
hollyhocks, marigolds,
my ancestry in lemons,
apples, amber.

Paris was my wildfire contagion
asparagus and melon at the bistros,
thunderstorms of invention
brewing in the galleries.
Rilke liked my studio filled with lilies.
I liked my studio red-striped
in between testaments of turquoise
and navy blue.

But it was my nudity
in self-portrait,
barometer of my becoming,
each portrait my private
cave wall, each brushstroke
trailing particles
of voluptuous gaze
from me in back silver.

Skulled fiddler at my bedside
the last weeks of my life,
baby daughter at my breast
while I exhaled Cezanne,
inhaled Gauguin, the staircase
they illuminated for me.

Who can ever take credit
for doing something first.
A pity my last-breath
pact between art and sorrow
between nascent soul
and shadow dancer.

How to Cohabitate with a Kaleidoscope

after Infinity Mirrors by Yayoi Kusama
Cleveland Museum of Art; 2018

arthropod eyes for equilibrium polka dots eye you as you eye them in your endless chamber sliver balls float among the hosta in this hot house mirror mirrored door claims you shuts you in she promises *in a most animated manner* modest proscenium launches you into the pleats and folds of abyss flickering gold lanterns dangling crystals polymath for your sensory pilgrimage cloth organs swim in the effervescence ain't no peep show but a long long story that refracts your body melts you away into the infinite spread tentacles bedazzle in ambrosia of space-time kabocha squash like paper lanterns guide your ancestors back to you on the gleaming waters of today's dream stars scatter like sugar another glitterbomb and then another another tumble spin fractal patterns you breathe in pulse with moments of
symmetry symmetry

In the Company of Flowers

> after Rebecca Louise Law's installation, *Community*
> at the Toledo Museum of Art

Submerge me into this linear bouquet
        curtains of plants
                      trickling down from heaven's grid
rack my focus through the rain
                              of rhythmic notations
        vertical riffs of
            ancestral petals
            tiny gourds on tender
            edge of rattle
            little swords of wheat
            fuzzy-hearted commas
            of whispery fronds
    all in a marimba of alchemy
to galvanize this womb of a room into pastoral idyll
                        selfie travelers transform
        become selfless
            revere pigtails of copper wiring
              chimes of gloriosa daisies
                blue larkspur
            lavender pulse of little lottie
  memories of love or loss try me on
                    nooks and crannies air-born staccato
            shadows harmonize with white walls
        membranes waltz onto linoleum floor
            yawning of dawn in low hum
                    the dead never so fresh & syncopated.

Launchpads

Before he died at the age of thirty-one in a fire in Amsterdam, Donald Evans had painted and catalogued almost four thousand stamps…issued by forty-two countries he conjured in his imagination.

Willy Eisenhart, *The World of Donald Evans*

So much seemed to depend
upon your chickens, each
of their many breeds praised
within perforated borders
of your miniature worlds.

Spider sense of rhythm
in your catalogues, your
autobiography crosshatched &
postmarked onto tiny ledges of
plot. You cradled gallery exhibits

under your arm & tempered
your philatelic obsession
with melancholy climates &
currencies rendered like jewels—
of plovers' eggs, pears, or

meadow mushrooms, kingdoms
of zeppelins, windmills, & staunch
minarets. Clouds notch your
ether, pronounce gold poppy,
painted trillium, grass-leaved

arrowhead, puffins in flight.
The mortar & pestle of
narrative clicks through
shadows obedient in sheet
after sheet of domino grids.

Your sable brush invented
paper joys, making us
believe in make-believe
as we still hover for nectar
from your lilliputian launchpads

that transport us to intricate
nowheres, issued, registered,
then cancelled—smoke vanquishing
your remaining lung, your ashes
pointillism atop an open sea.

Cinema Verite

You're away at work, teaching the rhetorical snarls of pathos while those cats of yours parade across the kitchen counter to lap up each crusty pool of creamed brandy and the salt from every stray peanut. Aerial shot of cat pee on the carpeting. Rorschach mystery. Which feline's mug to cut to? Horizontal pan: five sets of whiskers twitching. Audio: those vibrating larynxes. Dissolve into a Saturday breakfast of raw broccoli, chunks of chocolate and your Royal Model 10. Each key a clackety note. Mic those keys. A bit louder. Those strokes answer the jumbled nodes in your head--ingrown call and response. Morning TV rerunning: *What's it gonna be...the curtain or the money?* You claim your title: late bloomer—contorted vixen of your own poetics—squeezing through the labyrinths between multiple-choice choices. You choose the curtain like a Scarlett. Tight shot of refrigerator note clinging to a pizza shop magnet: *What's the big idea for today?* You think about it: a royal blue diary, a slip into the breaks of Coltrane who'll be honking with the sacred precision of a two-mile V of geese, a blackboard that lied all week about its greenness, a greenbrier to wish upon, that greenhorn who appears in your morning mirror. Your right foot begins the day's trudge that propels you into blur: congested currents of post office and bank, two-fisted laundromat, grocery cart with toothy mouth, lonely living room walls. Another dissolve. Closing scene under a stained quilt with curling cats, and *The Invisible Man's* scoop of vanilla ice cream steaming from the drizzles of warmed sloe gin. You close your eyes, thankful that Ben and Jerry don't have the literary gumption to co-opt it.

Double Feature

This Sunday morning is
my nursemaid whose

task will be to heal
creases of too many

mumbling nights.
Thunder claps and

snoring husband
prick the tender

skin of my arches,
rolls of rain stir

my spine. With
tented newspaper

atop her head, Memory
scurries inside for tuck

pointing. Shadow
returns worn and vatic.

\+

*Friday night
her lipsticked*

*mouth, laced
with sweat and*

*popcorn salt,
makes silly*

*sucking noises
as it quivers*

*over a ripening
in the backseat*

*of a mother's Saab.
On the other side*

*of the drive-in's
chain-link fence,*

*old man with
yellow-toothed*

*yawn greets a line
of steamed car*

windows. Gray strands
of his beard hover

in the hot breeze
as he trudges

through crushed beer
cans and exhausted

prophylactics towards light
from a giant screen. Sound

track swells. Bambi slams
a front door her shaky

hands latch six dead
bolts. Violins staccato,

close-up of mascara eyes
watering fear. Another

tight shot—her bare
shoulder, a hairy hand

cups the pulse of her
neck. Camera pans,

two shadows on the wall:
Bambi's curves, monster's

mass. Freeze frame.
Credits roll. Car, van,

truck doors open slam
shut. Snack bar

attendants at attention
behind battalions of

nacho plates. Onto
the bow of her upper

lip, she applies Angel
Red with painter's flair,

leaves to sweet talk chicken
nuggets and a cherry slush,

her tiger-print panties
dangling from a stick shift.

+

Fog cleaves, I pine for a
younger Shadow congealing—

homemade picture books
of childhood adventures,

canopy bed the secret sea
or space station fearless.

    +

She squats on the curb
that circles Concessions.

Underneath her floral skirt.
she pulls knees to chest

then slowly licks her fingers
after each greasy morsel

from a paper boat.
Commotion erupts,

two jocks from her school
wrestle the old man, press

him to his knees. "You pay
for it next time, asshole"

and a cellophane hoagie
propels through the air,

streamers of pink
milkshake its comet's

tail. The old man
rises, brushes dirt

from his pants, churns
fists into his pockets, wipes

his face and neck with
a wrinkled rag and sits

beside her. They share
a Lot-a-Gulp of cherry

cola and the back-and-forth
of small talk. He pulls a gold

charm from his pocket
size of a quarter attached

to a thin black cord. He rubs
off lint and places it in her

palm. She slips it over her
head and lets the amulet

fall between her breasts.
It is heat.

+

Memory a nesting doll
that taunts me with infinite

regression, rabbit holes of
narrative confection. Are

those apparitions or shadows
on weary walls of married life?

⠀⠀⠀⠀⠀+

Last forty of top
forty before

intermission ends.
His steel blue

eyes on her now.
Takes her hand.

His arm hooks
around her waist,

pulls her to him
breasts prickle

against his flesh
beard strokes

her cheek
her neck

his breath steamy
and salty; his growing

hardness pushes
against her. Guitar

riffs rise. They spin,
her skirt flutters

around his thighs,
her long curls caught

up in their vortex,
gyroscope possessed.

Bass lines tongue
her, Memory rattles

.

her, roller coaster
terror and her father's

arm too tight around
her shoulders. Stranger

breaks away, whirls,
twirls even faster.

A tornado of color
his arms propellers

then blast of air,
single column

of dust suspended
her damp hair

glistens. She shuts
her eyes, breath

lifts her once more
to the place where

she had been. Under
the yellow glow of

the concession stand,
she takes off amulet,

its soft tail drapes
over her fingers

and his scent of sulphur
wayward bound.

+

This Sunday morning
thunderstorm and ceiling

fan rhythm and the musk
of husband suspended

in sleep, the crust of
defeat sealing his eyes.

Landscape Decrees

> after Hiroshi Teshigahara's
> *Woman in the Dunes (1964)*

From rock to stone to sand we learn
to stagger breathing as we skim
across singing dunes improvising
maps like fishermen the shadows
of crows the moonlight that
licks patterns of our days
jeweled insects commune
with our knees, shins.

We crawl along the rocky
precipice just wide enough
for bellies the blueprint
of our snags and tears
the drop below is deep
we don't look down
our skin's parchment
may seal on its own.

Granules will be
our last witness
Delusion our
escort—plummet
or slow sink—

vision will take
us as light
subtracts first
from edges
horizontal
then
vertical
the law
of sand
& sentence.

Your Name Here
for Nina Paley's Sita Sings the Blues (2008)

Like the brand of preoccupation that thrives in dream
obedient constellations followed a crescent moon
glissading across the lip of a wall until
you pulled from your mouth a thread
with sewing needles dangling,
and your monkey warriors v-shaped
across the lake.

Your canonical path in squigglevision,
your many-faced face refracts
like a funhouse mirror while
cutout shadow puppets telegraph me
warnings. If you fling my heart
into a steel basin, it will continue
beating for a few minutes so please
don't take it till it's still, and bury
my body in the peat face up
my jewelry dropped
along the way.

Madame Curie's tubes glowed like faint
fairy lights, her journals radioactive.
Not me with my dollar store flashlight
tracking invisible salamanders in the woods,
the handlebars of my pink and white

Schwinn festooned with bluebells
from gardens that never existed,
my head tucked under my wing.

I'm in a clown car of predicament,
globe spins inside my belly while
your tweedy dourness sublets me
and I don't know what to do with
my hands. I am pickled in the rules
of your story world, I am your set
of parentheses, the low drama
of your furniture, all sanitized
for your protection which leaves me
waiting for the signal posts to light:
me oh my/my oh me.

Appetizers for Lunch

Same booth. Same song…Same sauce—sweet and sour.
Miss Kubelik in *The Apartment* (1960)

Billy Wilder lurks behind the palm trees
near the booths in the Kauai Garden;
tiny frogs perched between his teeth.
Suits and tight dresses rendezvous in
as many dirty fairy tales as the place
can hold. Dialogues swim in their own
ellipses. Mai tais hold all the cards.
Don't blame Hugh Hefner for these
scenarios. He was just America's Fuller
Brush Man bringing it to the door.

Ginger Rogers' Feathered Gown

mothballs don't suit me
                and I probably deserve hell
      ostriches plucked   bloody and raw
yet if you squint beyond the celluloid
              gently I will lift you
      onto an aqua cloud
                          and Fred will evaporate
while you float   with me
                        and Ginger
                                a s w a n s e d u c e d

        spinning like sugar

                        shimmering across white satin

              imagine your cheek

                      caressed by my tender plumage

    I will dip you

             into honeyed meringue

                    I will make you

                            surrender to divinity
        I am the dress that will survive you all

Mon Oncle Aussi
for Jacques Tati

Your movies—amusement parks in the mute lexicon of
wit, each gag triumphant like an erector set detonating
titter & yowl to stir my blood and get me pondering the

slow burn and contours of my life's punchlines. I want
you to be my very own Uncle Hulot, your gangly cartel
of a gait kicking up visual puns so pure—your stunted

fedora, wrinkled trenchcoat, tongue of a pipe, thesaurus
of classic acrobat and mime. I adore the sudden angles of
your rooster walk, your jig jag journeys, the 70 mm full-

framed ballets of colliding cross-purpose, your goofy
doohickeys of modern gadgetry then beguiling us with
sunlight upon the aria of a canary caged. Your dialogue

often dormant, your sound effects had wings, you knew
how to play with the sonic of things—nuances in the click
or thud of footsteps, a chair cushion that exhaled like a horse.

Your couple rolling like eyeballs along the circular rims
of their second-floor windows makes me want to swell
my gaze. How might I rewind/rewrite my scenes for

better payoffs—lean in for the turntable's nudging,
mirror my geography beyond the frame, keep my tail
wagging on another paved path that curls unto itself.

Wig of the Bride of Frankenstein

That wasn't the end at all…imagine yourselves standing by the wreckage of the mill.
                        Mary Shelley to Lord Bryon and Percy Shelley
                        Bride of Frankenstein (1935)

My Depression era stopgap

My sequel stellar

My genre playroom

My silver-streaked testimony

My drag queen minions

My Hays code coding

My camp conquest

My no name naming

My Elsa uncredited

My teenage heart timpani

My seismic charge

My dazzling hilltop tower

My *kites were ready*

My long electrical shaft

My mummy birth

My close cut eyes

My demented doctor bridesmaids

My same sex parents

My *it's alive alive*

My Nefertiti echo

My beehive electric

My pompadour jazzed

My hairline caged
My no wig at all
My mouth wadded & stuffed
My robotic bird head
My jaw scar map
My baroque camera angles
My chiaroscuro gods
My screeches played backwards
My angry swan hiss
My *stronger than a pretty love story*
My refusal to comply
My wedding night imploded
My bride of fire
My imagine yourself standing by the wreckage of the moon
My *you know how lightning alarms me.*

The following poems, many appearing first in journals or anthologies, were then included in my previous full-length collections. Some have been revised for this volume:

Fishing for Rabbits. Boston, Massachusetts. Kattywompus Press. 2013

    "Dick & Jane, All Grown Up"
    "Lunch with My Analyst"
    "RE: Secretaries From Hell"
    "Fairy Tale"
    "Depending on a Definition of What Is Is"
    "You Can Call It"
    "Charles Darwin at the Beagle Point Mall"
    "Baroness Elsa's Dinner Party"
    "Literary Movement: An Answer Key"
    "'Spring Fashion Modeled by Rising Young Poets'"
    "Cinema Verite"

Make Me That Happy. Elyria, Ohio NightBallet Press. 2017.

    "Star Virus"
    "What's With My Inner Zombie"
    "The Man of Ice Cream"
    "Museum of His Bumper Stickers"
    "Taxidermy for Erotica"
    "Resharpening the Interim"
    "Probabilities: An Inventory"
    "Villanelle Sonic"
    "Codifier"
    "Deep As It Is Narrow"

"Follow Him"
"'A Swift and Fatal Plunge, And Then the Abyss of Sorrow'"
"Andy Warhol's Buffet of Thoughts at the Kahiki Supper Club"
"Arguments for Furniture"
"Still Life with Whoopie Cushion"
"This Space Reserved"
"Double Feature"

Dodge, Tuck, Roll. Parma, Ohio. Crisis Chronicles Press. 2018

"Betty Boop Drops the Mic"
"Betty Tosses Her Stilletos…"
"Betty Marries Herself"
"Blue"
"Midnight Wife Sleeping"
"Wardrobe Conditional"
"Curate This"
"When Sit Means Sit"
"Thin Lines"
"In the Face of Another International Asteroid Day"
"Stephen Hawking Throws a Soiree for Time Travelers But This Time, They Show Up"
"7th Son"
"Dining with Picasso"
"John Cage Reconsiders Harmony"
"More Than They Should"
"New Republic Princess"
"Woman Painting Women"
"Landscape Decrees"
"Your Name Here"

Rikki Santer has worked as a journalist, a magazine and book editor, co-founder and managing editor of an alternative city newspaper in Cleveland, Ohio and a poet-in-the schools. She earned a M.A. degree in journalism from Kent State University and a M.F.A. degree in creative writing from The Ohio State University. Her work has won honors from The Poetry Forum (the William Redding Memorial Contest), Black Lawrence Press (the St. Lawrence Book Award Competition), the Ohio Poetry Association, the National Federation of State Poetry Societies, the Best of Ohio Writer Contest sponsored by the Poets' & Writers' League of Greater Cleveland, as well as four Pushcart and three Ohioana Book Award nominations, and a fellowship from the National Endowment for the Humanities. Two of her published poetry collections have explored place: *Front Nine* (the Hopewell earthworks of Newark, Ohio) and *Kahiki Redux* (the late Kahiki Supper Club of Columbus, Ohio). *Clothesline Logic* was published by Pudding House as finalist in their national chapbook competition. She also has published three full-length collections: *Fishing for Rabbits* (Kattywompus Press), *Make Me That Happy* (NightBallet Press) and *Dodge, Tuck, Roll* (Crisis Chronicles Press). She and her artist husband live on a wooded ravine in Columbus, Ohio. You can contact her through her website: www.rikkisanter.com

Other books by Rikki Santer:

Front Nine: A Biography of Place
Clothesline Logic
Kahiki Redux
Fishing for Rabbits
Make Me That Happy
Dodge, Tuck, Roll

www.ingramcontent.com/pod-product-compliance
Lightning Source LLC
Chambersburg PA
CBHW030118100526
44591CB00009B/449